Not what I thought.

Skyler Anderson

BookLeaf
Publishing

Presentation by *BookLeaf Publishing*

Web: www.bookleafpub.com

E-mail: info@bookleafpub.com

ISBN: 9789395620987

First edition 2022

DEDICATION

Dedicated to M&M.

ACKNOWLEDGEMENT

Thank you to them. The ones I had to leave behind but pushed me to become who I am. I may not be perfect, but I am who I am.

Thank you to the ones who stayed. Thank you the people who gave me an opportunity to create these poems. Thank you to the company who gave me a chance.

Thank you to my kids, Maya and Miles. My M&Ms, the pushing force for anything I do anymore.

PREFACE

Hey, thanks for taking the time to pick up this piece of myself. Some of these poems come from my own trials, some come from fun prompts. I hope these, if even just one, helps you the same way they helped me during their creation.

If you are having troubles, remember you are not alone. Someone wants you, someone cares for you. You've changed my life just by taking the time to read my poems. So thank you, from the depths of my soul.

If you aren't, thank you for taking the time to learn more about another person. To try to exist in their world, to understand their view.

The Shelf

Did you flourish?
Did you grow?
This time you took away from earth
As if you were the only one who felt any hurt

Returning yourself to the shelf
Turning away from the ones who help
To answer any questions with a relentless
I don't know.

Just tell me.
Did you flourish?
Did you grow?

Can I flourish?
Can I grow?

If I make myself better
In any kind of weather
Then will you want who I am?
Do you want my cardiogram?

Watch every beat of my heart
For your own safety
Your own concern.
Not wanting to know

Did I flourish,
Did I grow.

The Ballad of a Man of
Music But No Band Part One

Times without music become left behind
No history or rhythm
To remind of past times
But what of a man of music and cheer
But without a band playing
Does that mean no ear
Will pick up his music?
Well, don't fear
The story is here.

You see, I knew a man,
A man without band
I lent him my ear,
for it was music I could hear
The man said his name
It danced on the wind
No glory or fame
Just a man with his name
On the corner, No shame.
He spoke his tales first
Finding his ground
His stories were bold
Full of life and sound
But he sung his stories on the streets

Using the sounds of what was around

No instruments, no microphones
Only natural music accompanied him down
Down the tales of his life
Down the tales he would witness
Watching from the sides
Sometimes with his
Book in hand, writing
Sometimes just listening
But every time he was stealing
Stealing these things
These things he was witnessing.

He needed no music
He needed no fame
I forget now but,
I know he told me his name
But maybe the man without a band
Is exactly what he is
Needs no more a name than the music
Which he rightly didn't need
Music may have distracted this man
This man without band
But when he turned around,
I saw the guitar in his hands.

Adult Wizardry

I don't feel like a kid anymore.
I'm not quite sure how it happened.
Or when.
All I know is that magic is gone.

Bubbles no longer mysterious
Mountains no longer just hear us
There is a new form of magic
One palpable
And much more dangerous

And this rips our youth away
This infernal adult wizardry
And it's installed inside of me

Has been growing for years
This desire for money and power
Instead of fun and flowers
It's only causing us tears

And we all say the same thing
We sit on the floor
And wish
Just let me be a kid a little more.

Safer in my Pocket

Do you know what you've done?
The surrounding cave is the one you designed.
These twists and turns, the nervous fun,
I tell myself to survive without the sun.

In the form of a person, a guide you may say.
I've found a route, one you didn't know exists.
They are in my same spot, the same kind of fray
Alive but covered in dismay.

This cave was designed to make us fail,
but in the end without this trap,
never would we have found this trail
This passage out, the safest path.

It may take time, and I'm willing to walk it.
There is nothing else I have to risk,
My heart is no longer in my chest,
It seems safer in my pocket.

What Does The Void Say?

Realizing the void has arrived
It's been you the entire time
Watching the black encompass

Everything.

Miasma-tic, it changes form from
Slapstick, to a hidden sense of humor
Tragic, this was never intended nor respected.

The darkness grew deeper as I grew older
Not realizing the depths to which I could be
dragged
Kicking and screaming
But also very willing
Watching you twist who I was
Into whatever it is I am now.

This time
The chaos is unstable
A situation unable
To be rectified.
It's the first time the void has opened
You didn't expect this
Voices silently, "show them, show HIM"

Like a demonic wisp, trying to be more

And I'm dying, coughing blood and phlegm.
The exit is near.
Just have to take this turn here.

Hidden Roses

Lipstick stains on her teeth
Reflects the stress in her mind
She feels tired, lonely and weak
Staring at the passing time

The bars have closed
The bed is numbing
No hidden roses
No one is coming

Is there a hope to end this hell
Finding "him", or who
But looking forever at something else
Something you never knew

Not just one but many fall
Showing perseverance
Until the perseverance drives us into a wall
A distant one, where no one can hear us

Finite/Infinite

Infinite existence
Tireless persistence
For the time we have here
We have created a sickness
One that leads us
Deceives us
We can waste it
Or we can let it bleed us
It causes us pain and pleasure
It may last forever
People think it's love
I think it's the weather.
This object is not of our design
And losing it could be considered a crime
We only have a finite amount of an infinite pool
Stop wasting all of my time.

I am now 30

Accepting time is an old concept.
Leaving behind what you held so dear.
Physically and mentally gripped with fear
But it doesn't stop

There are no choices
You hear the sadness
Hidden in the elder voices
The other half assuming their life
Will be different, fuck this strife
It doesn't work that way

Refusing to accept
Embracing it isn't easy either
Just as hard of a next step
"Older means wiser"
I've just rotated
Around the big sun 30 times
Should it be moderated
Created
Something syncopated
Happy birthday they say
Now that I'm dated
But alas it took time
If I stay here stagnated

My life leaves me behind
That's been demonstrated

Accepting isn't my way
I won't go easy, I'll finish my gripe
When it comes to this acceptance
DMZ, No fights.
Time and I will combine our efforts
That's the way this feels right.

The Immortal Promise

It's ok.

I promise going to be.

I just can't decide of who I'm convincing.

You or me.

The Ballad of a Man of Music but no Band Pt 2

I started the story of the man
The man with no band
But now I've seen
The guitar
The guitar in his hand

So I asked the Man of Music
You said you make none of your own
But I can see what your groping
The guitar is acoustic
The guitar that you holding

He replied in riddles, twists and things
Jokes and more
Laughing and grabbing
The guitar
The guitar….. is missing a string?

I looked closer and found
Even more riddles now
There are no string bound
On the guitar
The guitar cannot make a sound

As he saw me wonder and ponder his instrument
He looked ever closer at me
My question imminent
About the guitar
The guitar that is impotent

Why?

Midnight Ramblings

I'm telling you I've been through worse
Some kind of rhyme within an intangible verse
Something for your mind to hang onto
When I walk away from you

The song just makes you cry
But it isn't so bad
To be this sad
Because if you fell this far
It was from a star
You started so high

You're telling me you've had better
Packing the ugly sweater
The one we got for the Christmas party,
Where I filled up on that tart, he

He said
The song just makes you cry
But it isn't so bad
To be this sad
Because if you fell this far
It was from a star
You started so high and had
You been iron clad

You would have seen, being up that high
Meant that you were dead.

Couch Sleeping

Some days are easy, some are rough

Some days just step on you

Sometimes you wake up ready

Sometimes you think the whole night through

TV burning the opposite wall
While it shows drama and faux life
The time it steals, it steals in silence
Living your life in strife

But the TV reaches the nooks you have
Those created comforts as a kid
There is a feeling you feel, like home
Somehow a place that is now forbid

Directions are missing

I'm losing my mind
The direction is missing
I've followed directions
But I haven't been listening
I've listened to the teacher
But I haven't been taught
I've learned to think critically
But I've not had a thought

Am I stuck?
Is this life?
Is it full of this back and forth strife?
I need the man to start the ride again
Like a ferris wheel,
Or a merry-go-round,
I'm not sure I can hear the sound
Of the outside

Yet it still drowns any ruckus
That comes out of my mind.

Existence within reality

Dishes staining a perfect picture
Time existing around it still
My brain debating
Is it worth the time?

Living life against a scripture
Wondering if a god is real
Is he creating?
Is there a rhythm or a rhyme?

Seeing life as torture
Creates a cycle all will feel
Dragging yourself and waiting
For the side of the cycle you climb.

It's not your signature
That defines your will
It's the life and skills you've been curating
I promise, it will be fine.

Chest Pain

The pain in my chest should be from the smoke.
Not from remembering the last words we spoke.

My brain is tired from the lobes to the stem.
From over-revving the engine at 3 a.m.

Time chases away the allegory of interaction.
Revealing true intentions without distraction.

Thinking Slots

It's a painful way to live
In limbo
Like a wound from a shiv
Unexpected knife blow
It's not the waiting but the thoughts
Over filling the thinking slots
The one thing my brain is lacking
Is an extra spot
I've sat here for a long time before
Decisions
Divisions
Demolitions
Revisions
But my ticket is almost up
The conductor takes his toll
My fare is too expensive
Even as I fight for my goal

Return of Heartache

The witness to who you are
The way you felt
Was it a misplaced
Over zealous use of grace?

Elegant and dangerous
A line without an end
Worrisome and whole
But no longer a home

I thank you for your interest
But I'm asking you
Please keep your distance.

Title goes here

There are times I wonder what could have been
And other times I feel like I've solved the puzzle
That I've built quite the castle
From all this rubble
Were you worth it?
All the trouble?

The fantasies
Not asked by me
Normally such a travesty
Get me a coffee
And these days,

Make it a double.
You sat in my mind
Like if you moved it would have mattered
The worst part was you didn't need movement
Under you I was already shattered.

Phoenix Alight

Wired in, finding something different
No longer ignorant

To these advances
Taking chances

Never was my forte
But today?
Is it fair play?

One burnt Phoenix
With its bag of old tricks

Won't rise because of the old flame
But because of new players to this ancient game

The phoenix does this, not for the calamitous
rest
For own self interest, to become the best

It own purpose, no matter if it seems selfish
Mark the record, leave it blemished

The creature fights for it's life
Not to be left behind in the middle of the night.

A Man

A man defined is defined by himself
The definition
Is an amalgamation
Of the position
Of the man during the construction
Of his living self

Not how many men can you kill
What's the amount of currency
That I can see
A wristwatch without dignity
Without humility
Is like rolling without a hill

An activity for the mindless
Following to be one of the crowd
Included, but not allowed
To feel the clouds
Stuck on the ground
With everyone's distress

A man stands when he can
Becomes what he needs when he must
Soft at times, hard when needed
That's the man we need to trust

The Ballad of a Man of Music but no Band Pt 3

Why?

Why, I asked the man.
The guitar in your hand,
It has no strings.
You produce no music
Yet I have heard these things.
They sound like notes
Tones in the air
But the guitar cannot make them
Are they really there?

Am I losing it, old man?
He smiled at me gently
No, young boy, you're not going crazy
You see, I am presenting,
Presenting a tune
One for everyone
But for each one of you, very soon
You'll see it's for you

The song becomes what we need
We as a whole
But the singular person

Needs room to grow
So I play for them all, not just the commander
What's good for the goose
Is good for the gander

As he said that to me
My mind opened wide
Saw the ones I loved
And the ones I left behind
But now I also see the lessons
The lessons they taught
But it doesn't lessen
The way I am fraught
With learning this world
This possible hell

But the music this man makes
The music of a man with no band
Makes me feel like maybe
Maybe
This world isn't so bad